CW00864966

hiding
in
the
safety
of
things

John
Staunton

to **Sharon**
for her gentle strength
and selflessness

and to **Matilda** and **Woody**
for making my life
a great adventure

.

man|s worst friend

__we exist in the life
of man|s worst friend
howling & prowling
& shitting & pissing

fucking & farting
& bitching & whining
snotting & sneezing
& yapping & planning

peering in shop windows
& looking at nothing
sweating & saving
& working & suffering

|full of rubbish
& waste
from our soles
to our skull|

empty of feeling
& talking of weather
listening to everything
__& staying so dull

let us sit on the moon tonight

let us sit on the moon tonight
holding hands till morning light
you and me and me and you
and no one else will ever do

let me say this one more time
it|s you and yours and me and mine
when all that|s left is each to kill
and as for love__i|m waiting still

p.s.__
d.o.a. 51

overlooking her funeral
was unthinkable
the priestly proceedings
made sure of that
of what was unmissable

drinking to remember
to forget a past
that was an unwanted
present__

a lost reality
trapped between bars
__as silent dreams
fell nearer madness

found
stone cold sober
on a slab

now__who in hell
is mourning tonight

the fire within

only__
in repetitive regression
is this sleeping
sulking bud
of my damn depression

bursting__
from coal black night
to blood yolk sun
seesawing
swinging
winding and winding
to a whole new wheel
of a day

filled__
bottom to brim
with this grave feeling
of my life|s
everlasting
impermanence

o_emily
no__
hope is not
that
feathered thing
but simply
the buoy
__as a man
i cling__
to ride this raging storm

books

i love my books better
than i love you

_____

i want to eat my books
drink and fuck my books
read and talk to my books
sit and study and admire
my books__
look and listen and
learn from my books
smell and touch and
taste and feel and
take care of my books
__with my books
i am never lonely
never sad never lost
never empty__
hardbacks and softbacks
and manuals and annuals
and volumes and volumes
of diaries and jotters and
notebooks and notepads
and copybooks and
children|s books__
and albums and annals
of pictures and paintings
and poetry and novels
of people and places__
and fiction and faction
and films and articles
and sonnets and songs
and stories of love and
longing and life and
all styles and sorts
of rhymes and riddles
___answered

shadow of the dead

__the green fool
meditated_
[a polite word]
on our canal__
disliked and barred
from many a bar
a thinker__
[a polite word]
left sitting and
wallowing__
waiting for
a seat__

__with aul finnegan
half blind in his
good eye__
half pissed
for his best part__
half with it [and not
understood]
for his own good__
half read by same
needing to say__
i|ve read bloomin|
____ joyce

__and the quare fellow
writing and performing
for cause and affect__
drinking and fighting
[leaving few
sympathetic]
our own failing
and lamentable__
insulin|t diabetic__

to s__

you stir my sorrow
empty soul
you fulfil
my far away fancy

you possess my breath
my blood
my being

my entire reason
my purpose
my progression
is for you__

you protect
__i prosper
you console
__we belong

the perfect
complement
__each one
completed__

serious hemingway

such a ship
wrecked
old man

drowning
in a sea
of uncertainty

a bullet
proof__

writing bull
of a mortal

brain shocked
word tight
___sentenced

the crawling pain

my soul is staggering
alone in a swarm__
my mind springing
within a storm__

my eyes are bleeding
my heart is rapping
my thoughts are falling
to the floor__
decomposing at the core

the skull is open
to the air__
unhealed and real
uncovered and raw

it|s like i am dead
__but not dead
_____nor alive
but condemned
by my own freedom
existing__
__amidst nothingness

the happy death of reggie crumb

reggie crumb fell down a hole
he is not coming back up
7 days have since past
he looks up at the world sky
he felt wonderful_he has not
eaten_drank_nor read a book

people looked down on him
he peeped up_people cried
down at him_he laughed up
one person spat on reggie|s
smile_he wiped his face
__this was his day

the hole is about 14 foot
deep_mr crumb is about 4
foot tall_all the people are
of different heights
the sky is moving_reggie is
staying_this is his hole

he slung his bag of shit up
at the people_now he is happy
he is hungry_this is his new
home_the world sky is now
sunless_people are restless

__he pissed and fell asleep
his mother is dead_his father
is deceased_he longs to be
departed from all this duration
nothing is important
everything is meaningless

his life is empty and full
of disease_and is downright
as disposable as__
his last defecation_____

crudity of thought and emotion

my heart is slow
and low
with woe

my head is hurried
and studied
and worried

i am pained
perplexed
and perturbed

i cannot
relax__

my spirit is restless
and hopeless
and lifeless

so who the
fuck has
the time__

to be fucking
pleasant__
and fucking polite

the needless seed

she emerged as an unripe
babe from body cold
on unclean bed__
unfolded__removed
one blood black night
to mourn thereafter

she woke one sorrow
in the splinter
of a cheerless june
woed and wedded to
wretchedness__
talked till trees of oak
spoke__telling of a
death before a blooming
rise and the shooting
morrow of a sleeping
sulking bud__

she shaked up straight
spoiled and stained
shrugging her world
stealing time__
to catch__to swallow
__a petal__poisoned

__she leaved
winded and tame
amongst the shrubbery
weathered__with
falling tears she
fell_softly_slowly
__into winter

rover

i love my dead little goldfish
because i killed him
he looked so so very hungry
so i fed and i fed and i fed
and he ate and he ate and he ate
until_____
i thought he would be full

then he exploded

blood & milk

your child
is your offspring
often loved
too much
often disliked
not enough
often looked
upon as__
cute__cuddly
asleep__
often needing
too often__
leaving you
|a new mother|
old__
with nothing left
nor able to tell
wrong from
right__
leaving you
needing
to be alone__
and also loved
__too much

mother | lost in the post

house to house
england to
ireland__

ashes to dust
and time to
settle__

remembering
no urn
to mourn__

regretting
__a love
misplaced

life

__a load of
question
marks

with some
exclamation
marks

while we all
wait__

for the full stop

work_the refuge of the failed
|the bitter bird of old age|

a soul forged
+ mass produced in plastic

a brain boiled
+ constipated

subdulated
+ pinstriped

the treadmill shaping
half people

fightless
+ caged

defeathered
+_____fucked

the dead

men and women
are equal |indistinguishable|
one and other seen
as machines of appetite

the brain and aptitude
removed from the body
as a prime and predictable
hunger takes hold

grubsuckers__leeches
clinging to the very scaffold
of existence

fat forging fat__flesh covering
decaying organs__
caged__by the necessitatary
longing to be fed and watered

and animals we remain__
as the mealtimes and
the glut and selfish stuffing
of the faces continues

the brain sucked dry
a body sluggish and obese

the dead_____feeding

poetry is___

the rising
of the spirit
the forging
of the heart
the freeing
of the brain

the chasing
of the clouds
the melting
of the sun
the catching
of the rain

the shooting
of the flowers
the lightness
of the stars
the depthness
of the sea

the shielding
of the pain
the saving
of the soul
the making
of the unknown
_____known

that is___
poetry to me

to s__

the steadfastness
of your love__

the<gentle>strength
and loyalty
of your affection

__is the selflessness
which covers me

darkness perceptible

thunder and storms
precipitate
my days of decline

as lightning bolts
^^^^circuitously
through the jagged
mud_mad_mind

on a high | on a low
feeling happy | feeling bright

full of sadness | full of woe
another day | another night

i wondered lonely

is there anything
lovelier than_a tree
a cloud_a swallow_
& a host of daffodils

is there anything
lovelier than_a tree
a cloud_a swallow_
& a host of daffodils

is there anything
wearier than_poetry
a crowd_& swallowing
a heap of sleeping pills

writer|s block

____nothing2write
&nothing2teach
nothing2say
&nothing2preach
nothing2inform
&nothing2tell
nothing2express
&nothing2expel
nothing2produce
&nothing2create
nothing2print
&nothing2puncuate

some most days

_____somemostdays i want 2
jump out of a basement window
somemostdays i want 2
cut my wrists with a blade of grass
somemostdays i want 2
take an overdose of multivitamins
somemostdays i want 2
put my head in an oven with a gasmask
somemostdays i want 2
lie down on a disused train track
somemostdays i want 2
hang myself with an elastic band
somemostdays i want 2
shoot myself in the head with a |blank|
somemostdays i want 2
sink down deep in the shallow end

_____somemostdays i want 2
_____somemostdays i want 2
4 mostsomedays i need to

dumb blind eye of the world

beware
the gathering of the lame
beware
the half people
beware
the pansy puking poets

|the phoney word vomiters
of stale air and farts|

they are inbreeding
___and horny for fame

the junkyard

the gull & gill dribbly half_deads
the cum of the city
the afterbirth of the retarded

the scumfucks & poxbottles
the scaled & abridged people
with faces of wirewool and concrete

are__dumping & raping
building & shaping__a wasteland

remains

these dumb poems
roar

through the brain
mating

like cancer cells
waiting

to be silenced__
on your shelf of dust

sardines on a bus

as i sit
brainless in
other peoples
bumsweat
& brine__i
solely wish
for isolation

__to be
as useless &
numb__as
other peoples
bellybutton
fluff

soulsucker

your heavenly baby
extracting
bloodjuices
and milk

sipping and
sucking

sapping and
draining

mewling and
puking

extorting from its host
that infinite supply

of generosity and
endurance

the genius of the fool

with a 22 cent
plastic bag
over his head
he blocked out
the world

__every|day
every|thing
every|body
every|one__

and in|between
darkness
and light

__in|between
thought
and emotion

he found
simplicity
of the
unconscious

a melting of madness

i sense a buzzzing
__a drone drum
numbing__
dull>sharp<sting
to the brain
____splaaat

now i hear myself
think |ing
        of all things
        with wings|

of all things
inholy__
        and unsane

19_710 days

for 54
FUCK years
i|ve woke up
depressed

54 FUCK
years feeling
deathly__

54 FUCK
years out
of mind__

54
FUCK years
crawling
from a sick
bed

_____to a life

resigned

the realest reality of all

my brain so full of all and nothing
trying to control and understand
trying to grab that meaning
trying to hold on to that meaning
that one important thing__
|but everything seems all wrong|

they tell me all will be fine and well
they tell me to step back a little
they tell me to watch and listen a while
to do less and little of more of less
|but everything seems all wrong|

i have seen all the wondrous things
i have seen such events take hold__
i have looked into the far end of my life
and i understand_____that death
is really the realest reality of all

flesh eaters

___nesting
on rooftops
and gutters
they sit__

thriving on
the sludge
and neglect
of the city

shiting down
on the people

mating and
mutating

the pigeons
and rats

___waiting

to take over

homeless

__at 68
he slept
dreaming of heat
under the bridge

worn down
newspaper
shoes +
red wine
in a box

at 3am
he was discovered

covered

|in 4 degree burns
_70%
of his body|

2 poured the petrol
1 lit the match

the savage god

they had to hose
him off the tracks

put his shoes and
umbrella into
the coffin

just to make you feel

there was something
left of him

the old skin

her new grief
gazes into the
looking glass

shielding itself
from the glare
and sharpness
of the light__

her new face
shaping itself
into the mask

___reflecting
the setting right
of the old skin

every life

every baby
born__
every book
burnt__
every lie
lived__
every laugh
laboured__
every love
lost__
every bone
buried__
is
___all
|and only all|
of what we are

prissy wordpushers

that horrible
creative stage
can be found
in the worthless
and searching
of the wasted
and the dull__

that horrible
creative stage
can be found
in the nerves
of the raw torn
freaks with
their fat words
and waste__

that horrible
creative stage
can be found
in the hopeless
and destructive
rage__of the
infected and
prissy
wordpushers
of haste__

in the dark of the night

that turning and turning
and stirring in my bed
that shifting and shifting
the feeling of dread

that winding and winding
of the ceaseless pain
that twisting and twisting
of the damaged brain

that waiting and waiting
for the easing of the light
that suicide feeling in
the dark of the night

the same and the same
and the wasting of time
will be forever and always
and endlessly be mine

the lunatic of the crowd

the chit_drivelling babble
of the unwanted surrounds me
choking and slaughtering
my thoughts without care

the dam_bursting bullshit
of the madness of the crowd
overpowering and suffocating
my space and my air___

bile flooding from my stomach
thoughts scorching my brain
subterfuging my face into the skull
of a non metaphorical monkey

eating rusty nails

and so the artist sits
hammering away
chipping

carving a name
in the blank page

fingers bleeding
on a skeleton hand
hacking

impotent words
on the bloody page

seductive love of self hatred

i sleep well and good
in the solace and satisfaction
of my mishaps
and my mistakes

i feel snug and secure
in the comfort and control
of my regrets
and my regressions

but__

i need and demand
the evil and necessary
drink

to dull the feelings
____and oil the senses

hiding in the safety of things

__let us not hurt
too much
let us not cut
too deep

let us not ask
too much
let us not choose
to weep

o_let us be free
from such things

and hide

in the safety
of things__

unshutdownable genius

i wish for things to have
purpose
and no meaning

i wish for things to have
perception
and no reason

i wish to understand
things |only| differently

__down side up
front to back
right to left
outside in__

to exist in |only| empty space

in that knowing place
of unshutdownable genius

the lonely order of things

i create to put shape
to my confusion__

to cover up the reality
of things__
to shield from the pain
of things__
to correct the disorder
of things__

to stay truthful
to myself__

in the lonely shadow
of things__

the man who couldn|t cope with reality

billy chubb has cancer
of the prostate which
has spread to his bowel
and his liver [but he doesn|t
want to know about it]

billy chubb has never
woken up positive_he
suffers from panic attacks
and depression [but he doesn|t
want to know about it]

billy chubb does not read
newspapers or watch
television_he hears bad news
on the radio [but he doesn|t
want to know about it]

billy chubb was told his
mother died 18 years ago_he
was taken away_and the house
was boarded up [but he doesn|t
want to know about it]

the way all things are

_____why o why
do all things die

frogs and cats
and mice and men

bees and fish
and trees and foul

plants and eggs
and dogs and prigs

_____all things
all ways

      always die

belongings

obscured
and isolated

with all my
possessions

i hide in that

__snail
__safe
__shell

_____

as they
possess me

i will be there when you fall
|to apologise for pushing you|

i loved you
in the insecure
the uncertain
__the meek

i wanted you
in the vital
the essential
__the weak

you see__

my surprises
in life have been
no surprise

__only in size

a bewildered bladder of a brain
|slumbering in a piss pool of disgrace|

__here i remain

alive
and undead

bored
and unmoved

BUT__

someday

i will climb
out of this
DAMN hole

and swallow
this whole
world
_____whole

all the characters are gone

__crooked eye joe &
the hunchback of the flats
__frothy face frank
& the mongol twins
__larry the limp &
old armless don
__the midget sisters
&_____albino tom

all gone | all gone | all gone

sole protector of the wasps in my head

it will be known
and known
it will be

you are now
what you were
then__

and ever more
you shall
be__

my lover__
and sole protector

of the wasps in my head

some things shall never alter

some things should
never alter__
as the seasons fold
into seasons
and time turns
into old__

such things shall
never falter__
as my love for you
stays the same__
and all things have
turned into gold

secret of perfection

mindy has a full silver length mirror
to see the reflection of the reaction
of the food within her belly in rebellion

the food mindy eats may stay in her
bowel before leaving her body
__or may leave by her mouth
|she will decide|

the room has a pleasant smell
from a slow releasing mushroom shaped
air freshener that sits underneath
the mini snack bar and cocktail cabinet

when finished sitting mindy will apply
the apple perfumed double quilted
velvet soft pink paper
|if needed|

after putting the magazines away
mindy leaves__
|her tummy in turmoil|
she is always long___sometimes late

jewels + stone

christ is leading my lead heart
of iron and wrath
by calling: come come
leave this earthly place

come come to a place of roses
and vine__for eye for a tooth
in my tame garden
of untouched fruit
__and cabbages rotten

come come to where lion
and mutton lay
to where bats and ravens
read dog_eared paper
biblebacks in braille

come come to a fairyland
of disabled faithless prigs
and hopeless poets
__forgotten

come come to an opening
of cheap red wine
|and everlasting harmony
__and devotion|
a haven__for spirit high
__on stale opium

faith and such

i need a religion
or something
as a refuge__
a supplementary
reality__

a place of blinkered
tranquillity__
and subsequent bliss

a place of
everlasting hope

__and mass
misunderstanding

nails in my coffin

to work is easy
__34 years easy

BUT__

to think AND work
the *same* 34 years
__is hard

HARDER__than
the fuking vinegar

christ had to drink
on his damn cross

my rainbows are in black & white

from a cotton cloud i fell
landed on a shit heap__
my mind pursuing poppies
my heart wrapped within
a crown of plastic thorns

i have a sadness that embraces
the stinking_smothering
soul_with such a satisfaction

i have a house |a crypt|
a garden |a graveyard|
a bed |a coffin|
a headboard |a tombstone|
a sheet |a shroud|
a body |a corpse|

i have a brain |open and raw|
in a bell jar view__
and a skull |cracked mess|
of an unclear pain__

i have all this
|in my hopelessness|
_____
and more

remains in black refuse
|a breakup|

blood runs deep
from a heart of stone
tears fall and weep
to chill the bone

the heart in two
is left for one
for what|s to do
when past is done

too long to live
when meant to die
too late to give
when meant to cry

a pain sustains
each broken vow
for what remains
is here and now

and all shall tell
what love is meant
for time to dwell
is time well spent

broken__

seesawing
falling
an old woman
stitching

rocking
and calling
to a child
from a chair

slouched
and crippled
coughing
and spewing

confused
and crying
|in a crooked
shape|

__tissues
all wrinkled
and sinews
___all torn

submitting to the wild ocean suppressed

sitting by my window
still
i wonder__

with all this pain

why something
as clear as glass

can be plain
to all
but me
__to view

__in a room
filled with
fog filled
babble__

i have a notion
i can hear
the sea__

so far astray

my wild ocean
__suppressed

sane and sober

stupid drink
left dribbling
left over grey
moustache__

left dried
mixing colours
dyed__

leaving a man
needing to
shave__

to show
he has control
over his own
face__

to show he is
a man__

sane and sober

to w__
|a remarkable son|

you are your
mother__
wise beyond
age_and
intelligently
sensitive

you are your
father__
modestly
handsom__
and does not
suffer fools
happily

you are us
both__
and more

you are remarkable

and you are
uniquely__you

to m__
|a perfect daughter|

perfect in manner
in thought
in action

a daughter of wisdom
and talent
and goodness

__with a gentleness
of mind and heart

a perfect daughter
to be proud of
to look up to
__and learn from

a daughter
who is perfect
in all ways__

who is faultless
and who is loved
beyond words

expectation & loss

blood ran along
her inner legs
|not as one
twelfth of a year|

she was happy
freewheeling
to wed and glad
to be happy

a new love
to safeguard
|life was good
_____

too good|

she woke to be told
of a death__
and the purpose
of hope

the gathering

a city of a mass
of human insects
marching____

bug_eyed and
obedient

trying to buy
the illusion
of happiness

trying to save
the cardboard
soul__

trying to spend
the day
away__

trying to forgo
to forget__

everything
necessary
___and crucial

acceptance

as a world around me
proceeds in its own
reality and certitude
of notion

i struggle for solitude
in my confusion

a little raw creature

the skin peeled away
the naked bones visible

___obeying time
___obeying time

why i want to die

      _____7|45 i start off sick and then i cry and then in pain i stumble from my safe bed_i fumble and feel so very frail_dress in yesterdays clothes and stagger into the severely lit bathroom_i look and stare at the ugly face in my mirror_do not bother to brush my stained teeth__ sitting on the loo i try to think of what i ate yesterday_i probably just drank_i leave the lonely house at whatever time it is_the streets are filthy with rabble and rubbish_it must again be bin day_since a miniature brown and white barking mongrel bitch is ripping apart every black and blue refuse sack_whilst green immature adolescents scamper to school_and grey experienced adults tread to their toil_i stand waiting for death_or the 18 bus_whichever comes first_a blind unsightly specimen looks at me most mornings and says the same tedious thing_NOT A BAD DAY AS LONG AS IT DOESN|T RAIN_she gets to the bus stop last but always gets on first_she sits and i stand_i pay_she has some sort of handicapped or retarded pass_i wish that i was deaf_or she was dumb or dead_after what seems like a life sentence standing_i stop standing and start walking_ i need a little support_the blind thing always gets assistance_i feel exceedingly sick thinking of this new day_i am now near the place of my 8 hour working shift_time to stop feeling ill and coughing_time to say good morning and impersonate a person who is not only healthy but also happy to have a fulltime job with the all important wage at the end of the week_so i can just about buy food_pay the gas_the electricity_ the rent_and have enough money left for my bus fare for the inevitable soul destroying 40 hour week ahead_i enter the workplace and say good morning_do my duty and say nothing out of the ordinary or that may cause the other employees to think i am on the verge of suicide_ a breakdown_or even violent mass murder_i leave broken at 5 and wait in the drizzle and dark with all the other weary workers_and in a fatigued and mournful fashion i follow them to that place we call home_later due to severe depression_i do not eat_nor do i have the power left to feel positive_i just sit on the loo thinking_that i can no longer go through the motions_and wish with all my heart for something far greater than this day gone__
      _____7|45 i start of sick and then i cry and then in pain i stumble from my safe bed___

why i don|t want to die

      when somebody is dead they are finished
with everything_all the books_the ornaments_
the paintings_and the rest in pieces of their precious
belongings will be left to a child or other blood link_
|whether they want them or not| all the expense and pain
spent will be for your borrowed time only_time to leave
this life and become nothing for all eternity_let the family
put your clothes and other items into plastic bags_that
stuff is now only in the way_whoever is left must start a
brand new life with all new things_after all_all your
personal effects will be too much of a reminder for them_
now your children will want to have their own children and
your wife will probably want to marry again_your friends
at best will be old and frail and will not want to be reminded
of their own forthcoming death_so after the tea and the
ham and cheese sandwiches_they will be only too glad to
forget the few photos on display to show they cared_or to
show the unborn grandchildren what granddad looked like
before he was embalmed and put in the ground_your house
left maybe all paid for if you worked hard and long when you
were young and healthy_now it will be sold for something
bigger and better by the grownup offspring_somebody might
even need a suit or a pair of second hand leather shoes |if you
left a good willed wife behind she may have given them to
oxfam or some such other greedy establishment| there are a lot
of mean |not poor| size 9 people of medium build who will be
only too glad to walk around in your footsteps
|at a cheap price|
      it is all over now
except for the plastic flowers that remain in the rain
and the annual overpriced unread reminder in the daily rag

Printed in Great Britain
by Amazon